Cuida tus modales / Minding Our Manners

¡A compartir! / Let's Share!

Walter LaPlante
Traducido por Eida de la Vega

Gareth Stevens PUBLISHING

conceptos básicos

Compartir es dejar que los demás jueguen con tus juguetes.

Sharing is letting others take a turn playing with your toys and games.

Compartir puede ser difícil, pero es algo muy grato.

Sharing can be hard. However, it is a nice thing to do.

Una amiga te pide que la dejes jugar con tus juguetes. ¿La dejas?

Your friend asks to play with your toy. Do you let them?

¡Sí! Eso es compartir.

Yes! That is sharing.

¿Y si no quieres compartir?

What if you do not want to share?

Es posible que no quieras compartir ciertos juguetes.

You might want to keep toys that are special to you.

Piensa en cómo te
sientes cuando otros
no comparten.

Think how you feel
when others
do not share.

Puedes sentirte triste
y solo.

You might feel sad
and lonely.

Cuando compartes,
les demuestras
a las personas que
las aprecias.

Sharing shows people
you care about them.

Puedes turnarte para jugar, compartir las palomitas de maíz o dejar que otros se diviertan con tus juguetes.

You can take turns at a game, share your snack, or let others use a fun toy.

¡Si compartimos, todos podemos jugar juntos!

Sharing helps us all play together!

Please visit our website, www.garethstevens.com. For a free color catalog of all our high-quality books, call toll free 1-800-542-2595 or fax 1-877-542-2596.

Library of Congress Cataloging-in-Publication Data

LaPlante, Walter.
Let's Share! = ¡A compartir! / by Walter LaPlante.
p. cm. — (Minding Our Manners = Cuida tus modales)
Parallel title: Cuida tus modales.
In English and Spanish.
Includes index.
ISBN 978-1-4824-1737-1 (library binding)
1. Sharing — Juvenile literature. I. Title.
BJ1533.G4 L37 2015
177—d23

First Edition

Published in 2015 by
Gareth Stevens Publishing
111 East 14th Street, Suite 349
New York, NY 10003

Designer: Andrea Davison-Bartolotta
Editor: Kristen Rajczak
Spanish Translation: Eida de la Vega

Photo credits: Cover, p. 1 szefei/Shutterstock.com; p. 3 Aaron Belford/Shutterstock.com; p. 5 Dejan Ristovski/Shutterstock.com; p. 7 Ami Parikh/Shutterstock.com; p. 9 Jose Luis Pelaez/The Image Bank/ Getty Images; p. 11 Oleg Mikhaylov/Shutterstock.com; p. 13 bikeriderlondon/Shutterstock.com; p. 15 Ilike/Shutterstock.com; p. 17 RimDream/Shutterstock.com; p. 19 Jupiterimages/Stockbyte/ Getty Images; p. 21 Jupiterimages/Pixland/Thinkstock; p. 23 petrograd99/iStock/Thinkstock.

Printed in the United States of America

CPSIA compliance information: Batch #CW15GS: For further information contact Gareth Stevens, New York, New York at 1-800-542-2595.